RELEASE YOUR PAST

Operating in Faith & Moving Forward

DR. JESSE E. THOMAS

Editorial Director: Dr. Larry Keefauver

Printed in the United States of America.

Paperback ISBN-13: 978-1-6322-1874-2
Hard Cover ISBN-13: 978-1-6322-1875-9
eBook ISBN-13: 978-1-6322-1876-6

www.xulonpress.com

Dedication

Dedicated to my beautiful wife and children.
It's my prayer that God will reward your faithfulness and give you the
desires of your heart. I also would like to dedicate this book to everyone that
didn't let their past define their future.

Table of Contents

Introduction:
Release Your Past

In the book entitled "Your Best Life Now: 7 Steps to Living at Your Full Potential," author and pastor Joel Osteen expresses that being spiritually and mentally stuck, "Is when an individual is set in their ways, bound by their perspectives and stuck in their thinking."[1] This is to literally suggest to all of us that when a person is stagnant in their imagination then their reality becomes very dim. I must declare to you that before your reality happens, you should already see the manifestation in your mind. This is an indication that you are moving spiritually even before the physical can arrive.

> **"You can't depend on your eyes
> when your imagination is out of focus."
> – Mark Twain[2]**

In other words, you should be walking by faith and not by what you see. Your faith should overshadow the tests, trials, and tribulations of this world. I know you see wickedness and evil on every hand, but by faith you can stand on what the Word of God declares, "Fret not thyself because of evildoers. Neither be thy envious of the workers of iniquity, for they shall soon be cut down like green grass and whiter as the green herb" (Psalm 37:1-2 KJV).

You may be seeing your money depleting and you're doing everything you can to make your ends meet by stretching your checks from week to week, but by faith you can declare, "My God shall supply all of my needs according to His riches in Heaven" (paraphrase of Philippians 4:19).

In order to move from a place of being stuck, you have to exercise your faith and see things happening in your favor before God opens the door and lifts up the window. Your faith isn't predicated if He can do it, but your faith is steadfast in knowing that He's going to do it, and it doesn't matter when, how, where, or even why. You should rejoice in knowing that God won't keep you stuck in the predicament that you're in.

Before your feet can move, your faith has to move. Before your situation can move, your faith has to move. If you're tired of being stuck in your present circumstance and condition, then your faith is the key in starting the process.

> *By faith Abel offered unto God a more excellent sacrifice than Cain... By faith Enoch was translated that he should not see death... By faith, Noah prepared the Ark... By faith, Abraham went into a land that he knew not. By faith, Sarah received strength to believe the promise of God to give birth pass her childbearing days.* (Hebrews 11:4, 5, 7, 8, 11 KJV).

This "Release Your Past" message isn't for everyone. But if you are tired of being stuck in depression,

    stuck in stress,

        stuck in debt,

            stuck with low self-esteem,

                stuck in sickness, and

                    stuck in bondage...then get up!

Get up and praise God...

In fact, you will discover that when you GET UP, you will also have the power to *LOOK UP!,*

        PRAY UP!

           PRAISE UP!

              POWER UP!

                PROGRESS UP!

                  PULL & PUSH UP!

Ready? Then get ready to release your past and start moving forward!

Chapter 1

Guilty of Being Stuck

"The only difference between a rut and a grave
are the dimensions."
-Ellen Glasgow[3]

M oses and the Children of Israel had been under the oppression
and rule of Pharaoh and feeling stuck.

*During the night Pharaoh summoned Moses and Aaron
and said, "Up! Leave my people, you and the Israelites! Go,
worship the LORD as you have requested. Take your flocks
and herds, as you have said, and go. And also bless me."*
(Exodus 12:31-32 NIV)

The Bible says that God touched the heart of Pharaoh to let His children go. This is a very important scripture to highlight in your Bible. We have too many people trying to change their enemies and change their naysayers, but this text gives us the blueprint on how to handle our enemies and haters. It's really a simple process so please don't miss it.

◇◇◇

Let God touch your enemy's hearts.

◇◇◇

When God touches their hearts, they'll have no other option, but to let you go. You may be wondering, how are they going to let you go. They'll have to let you go when their heart is touched by God. God will touch their hearts and have them speaking to you when they don't want to. God will touch their hearts and they'll have to sit at tables that God has prepared for you. God will touch your haters heart and they'll have to witness the blessings that God has for you. Your haters can't block what God has for you. Your haters can't stop it. You must understand, what God has for you it is for you! So, instead of running your haters and enemies away, pray for God to touch the hearts of your haters. Don't pray for God to remove them, just pray that their hearts are touched by Him. When God touches their hearts, He will allow your enemies to see the next blessing that God has in store for you.

However, as the children of Israel are fleeing from Egypt, they are still in the boundaries of Egypt. They flee a place of bondage only to find more challenges before them. After Pharaoh releases the children of Israel, he sees that they aren't returning. So now, Pharaoh makes a mandate to go find the children of Israel and bring them back into bondage. That's how the adversary works. When the enemy sees that you can make it without him, he will try to make you return. That's why you don't need to respond to every text message. It's just the enemy trying to make you return. You don't need to answer every email in your inbox. Be aware that the enemy is trying to make you return. You have to get rid of that scent in your nose of the past because the enemy will try to make you return.

So, Pharaoh tries to enslave the children of Israel again. The text says that while they are traveling from Egypt, they get mad at Moses because things aren't quite working in their favor. In fact, they get upset with

Moses and ask Moses the question, "Why did you bring us out here in the first place to die? Is it because they didn't have any graves in Egypt?" So, now they find themselves at a place of being stuck.

Why Are They Stuck?

They are guilty of being stuck because of the wilderness around them. The text says that they flee Egypt, but they are still in the boundaries of Egypt. This simply shows us that God will allow us to only go so far in order to keep the focus on His promise and not our problems. The promise was made to Moses, but the problem is the children are complaining to Moses about what they see and they forgot about what God said.

I want to suggest to you as you're reading this to stop focusing on the wilderness around you. The wilderness is only to keep you focused on the promises of God. Your wilderness could be pain and heartache, but it's to keep you focused on God's promise. God promised to never leave you nor forsake you. Your wilderness could be a sickness in your body, but I tell you to focus on the promise. The promise is, by His stripes, you're already healed.

Not only is the wilderness around them, but they have the world against them. The text says that *Pharaoh is behind them*. Pharaoh is a representation of what the world consists of—Deception, Depression, Envy, Hate, Jealousy, and Confusion. All of these worldly weapons are against you, but just like the children of Israel, God told Moses, "I'll take care of Pharaoh; you just keep moving." No matter what may be against you, God says you don't have to remain stuck. Just let Him handle it and you keep moving. I remember writing a song entitled, "Move Satan." Sometimes, you have to make a declaration and tell the enemy, "Move out of my way! Get out of my family! Get out of my relationships! Get out of my finances! Move!"

In order to move the enemy out of your way, you must move out of your rut and get unstuck. How does that happen? *Moving* requires you to start. Now, that's obvious but not easy. Here is a question that I believe we must consider in order to move forward and get unstuck. Consider what is keeping you from moving forward. Check off any inertia indicators below that are hindering or blocking your movement:

- ☐ Fear
- ☐ Fatigue
- ☐ Lack of motivation
- ☐ Lack of confidence
- ☐ Apathy
- ☐ Critics and enemies surrounding you
- ☐ Ignorance
- ☐ Addiction
- ☐ Abuse
- ☐ Prayerlessness
- ☐ Faithlessness
- ☐ Believing lies
- ☐ Toxic Relationships

Now, let's discover how to move ahead.

Move Through What's Ahead of You

Not only do the Israelites have the wilderness around them, the world against them, but they have the water ahead of them.

Moses asks God, "What are we going to do now with this water ahead of us?"

God answered, "Look in your hand. Take your rod and what you used for yourself, I'm giving you the opportunity now to use it to help somebody else." We read that when Moses lifted his rod the waters began to divide and the Israelites went through the sea on dry ground, with a wall of water on their right and a wall of water on their left.

> *Then the L*ORD *said to Moses, "Why are you crying out to me? Tell the Israelites to move on. Raise your staff and stretch out your hand over the sea to divide the water so that the Israelites can go through the sea on dry ground. I will harden the hearts of the Egyptians so that they will go in after them. And I will gain glory through Pharaoh and all his army, through his chariots and his horsemen. The Egyptians will know that I am the L*ORD *when I gain glory through Pharaoh, his chariots and his horsemen."* (Exodus 14:15-18 NIV)

Yes, there will be trials ahead of you, but you don't have to let them keep you stuck. God not only commands you to move, He also gives you the power, strength and courage to MOVE! Robert Schuller's famous line for this is:

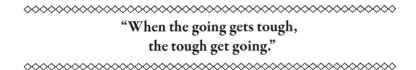

**"When the going gets tough,
the tough get going."**

Staying stuck is a choice; getting unstuck and moving through the trials, tribulations and tough obstacles ahead is also a choice. Get over your procrastination and pride...*ask for help from God and from godly people around you.* The army of God, saints and believers in His Church, are ready to help you fight. When the pain of being stuck becomes greater than the fear of exposure, you will reach out for help. There is no shame in needing a helping hand from the family of God.

Do you remember the friends who took their crippled friend to Jesus? Jesus was inside of the house. The place was so crowded that the friends of the crippled man, lifted him up on the roof, created an opening, and lifted him down into the room in front of Jesus. The condition you are in right now isn't as crippling as you think it is. You have more help than you could imagine. Make a list of those around you who trust Christ, who love God, and love you. Ask for help! Moses and the Israelites helped one another move through.

Also, understand that you can help others who are stuck. God is saying to take something you have used for yourself and use the wisdom, knowledge, and understanding you have acquired to help someone else. These hands you have used for yourself are now to LIFT UP and bring healing and help to others.

Agree with God to get up and move forward...and break through any obstacles before you. God and His people will walk you through. God is giving you a divine appointment and opportunity to help you from getting stuck. Your stuck days are over. Keep moving. God will empower and embolden you to walk through warfare that should have destroyed you. The heavenly and earthly armies of God are for you...so who can be against you?

Moments of Release

At the end of each chapter, I will offer you an opportunity to begin to apply the truths from God's Word to your own situations. Take the time to go through this section before you move onto the next chapter. Today, begin to move forward and overcome those things that are trying to keep you stuck in a rut by standing on His promises.

If you are tired of functioning while being fractured in your present circumstance and condition, then your faith is the key in starting the process. In order to move from a place of being fractured, you have to exercise your faith and see things happening in your favor.

What instruction promise are you given in Philippians 4:19?

What blueprint did this chapter reveal on how to handle your enemies?

Stop focusing on the wilderness around you. Begin to focus on His promise. Begin by meditating on these promises: [Look up each verse; write it down; memorize it; act upon it!]

John 16:33
Romans 8:31
Isaiah 54:17
Romans 9:33
1 Peter 2:24
James 4:7

No matter what may be against you, God commands you to get unstuck. Just let Him lead you through and keep you moving.

Make this declaration:

Satan, I rebuke you in the name of Jesus.
 Get out of my family! Get out of my relationships!
  Get out of your finances!
Jesus Christ, I give you all praise, glory, and thanksgiving,
 for the coming victories you have already won for me!

Make a to-do list of ways you will use your hands and the tools God has given you to bring help, healing and blessings to others. Remember, the spiritual gifts the Spirit has given you are not for you…they are for ministering to others!

Meditate on and Memorize:

> *And my God will meet all your needs according to the riches of his glory in Christ Jesus.* (Philippians 4:19 NIV)

Thank God for this promise.

Chapter 2

3 Steps Up

Look Up: Aware

    Get Up: Arise–Move Forward One Step at a Time

        Stay Up: Act – Keep Focused, Stay in the Good Fight, & Finish Strong

"Somewhere along the way we must learn that there is nothing greater than to do something for others."–Dr. Martin Luther King, Jr.[4]

I think we can all agree that there aren't a lot of things you can do that can match the feeling you get when you help someone in some positive way. In fact, we're all experiencing this thing called **"Life"** together and as you know, life isn't always an enjoyable ride. You'll have some ups and you'll have some downs. You'll have moments of laughter and you'll experience moments of shedding tears. You'll have moments where you'll want to be around family and friends and then you'll have times in your life in which you just don't want to be bothered. Sometimes, life has a way of making you feel helpless.

Actually, life can make you feel so helpless by draining you mentally, spiritually, and physically. The time will come when you'll find yourself needing help in life, or even looking for an opportunity. If you can be honest sometimes, you just need someone to show you some compassion and kindness. If you had someone to help you in some way, you should remember how it felt and keep that same feeling in your mind when the opportunity arrives for you to help someone else. I don't know about you, but I know how it feels to receive help when you need it.

You may remember how it felt when helped arrived in your situation. Maybe you were broke, busted, and bitter, but help showed up. You may remember the time when your car wouldn't start or you didn't have a car, but help showed up. You might recall not having enough money for all the bills, but somehow and someway help showed up. Perhaps, you did not have a job to go to, but help showed up and you haven't missed a beat since being unemployed. You may have been sick and not knowing how or when you were going to get well, but help showed up and touched your body. So, if you know it feels to receive help, then you should be willing to help somebody else.

◇◇◇

"If I can help somebody, as I travel along;
If I can help somebody, with a word or song;
If I can help somebody, from doing wrong,
then my living shall not be in vain."
– Mahalia Jackson[5]

◇◇◇

Let it be your good deed to encourage someone by way of a phone call, text message, or even a social media post by telling them you know how it feels when you are at your wits' end and help shows up. Tell them to hold on and don't give up because help is on the way.

In Luke chapter 5, it talks about the mission and ministry of Jesus Christ. Jesus is preaching from the seashore and people are gathering by multitudes to hear what He has to say. The Bible informs us that the word is spreading so rapidly, that Jesus goes from the seashore and gets in the boat to teach to the massive crowd. He no longer blends in with the crowd, but the Word steps out.

Stop for a moment and think about how this exemplifies that you aren't called to blend in. You are called to stand out and declare the truth of God's Word especially in times of chaos and confusion. You are called to be different. You can't be focused on being liked and talked about, but you have to have the mindset to do the work and will of God. This may require you to stand up and step away from the crowd.

> *When he had finished speaking, he said to Simon, "Put out into deep water, and let down the nets for a catch."*
> *Simon answered, "Master, we've worked hard all night and haven't caught anything. But because you say so, I will let down the nets."*
> *When they had done so, they caught such a large number of fish that their nets began to break. So they signaled their partners in the other boat to come and help them, and they came and filled both boats so full that they began to sink. When Simon Peter saw this, he fell at Jesus' knees and said, "Go away from me, Lord; I am a sinful man!" For he and all his companions were astonished at the catch of fish they had taken, and so were James and John, the sons of Zebedee, Simon's partners.*

Then Jesus said to Simon, "Don't be afraid; from now on you
will fish for people." So they pulled their boats up on shore,
left everything and followed him. (Luke 5:4-11 NIV)

Jesus tests the faith of His disciples who had been fishing, but had not
caught any fish, although they were professional fishermen. They were in
a position of needing help. Peter tells Jesus that they had been fishing all
night and had not caught anything. Jesus tells Peter to cast his net on the
right side of the boat and he would get what he needed. Peter follows the
instruction of Jesus. As a result of Peter's obedience in a time of needing
help, not only did Peter get what he needed, but he also experienced an
overflow. The Bible says that Peter had to get his partners to help pull in
the fish because it was too much for their boat.

When you obey God, He'll give you more than you can handle. In fact,
God said, in your moment of need, because you obeyed His voice, your
blessing is going to be so great you're going to have to share the overflow
with those that are connected to you. Your children better get ready! Your
family better get ready! Your best friend better get ready! Your co-workers
better get ready, because God said, "You've been in need too long for Me
not to bless you and those that are connected to you."

While Jesus was in one of the towns, a man came along who
was covered with leprosy. When he saw Jesus, he fell with his
face to the ground and begged him, "Lord, if you are willing,
you can make me clean."

Jesus reached out his hand and touched the man. "I am
willing," he said. "Be clean!" And immediately the lep-
rosy left him.

Then Jesus ordered him, "Don't tell anyone, but go, show yourself to the priest and offer the sacrifices that Moses commanded for your cleansing, as a testimony to them." Yet the news about him spread all the more, so that crowds of people came to hear him and to be healed of their sicknesses. (Luke 5:12-15 NIV)

Jesus then moves along and is approached with another circumstance of someone needing help. The Bible says that a man with leprosy sees Jesus and falls down in prayer. Jesus reached out His hand and touched the man and immediately the leprosy left his body. He told the man go and don't tell anyone what has happened to you, but the man couldn't keep it to himself. The man went and told everyone about what happened to him and everybody came to listen to what Jesus had to say.

Jesus finds Himself before a large crowd after helping Peter, his partners, and the man with leprosy and another opportunity to help somebody.

One day Jesus was teaching, and Pharisees and teachers of the law were sitting there. They had come from every village of Galilee and from Judea and Jerusalem. And the power of the Lord was with Jesus to heal the sick. Some men came carrying a paralyzed man on a mat and tried to take him into the house to lay him before Jesus. When they could not find a way to do this because of the crowd, they went up on the roof and lowered him on his mat through the tiles into the middle of the crowd, right in front of Jesus. When Jesus saw their faith, he said, "Friend, your sins are forgiven." (Luke 5:17-20 MSG)

Four men came bringing a paralytic man on a stretcher. The problem was the men couldn't get to Jesus because there were some obstacles standing before them. Whenever you have the mindset to get to Jesus or to be in His presence, you must understand that the enemy will always try to block your progression. Your obstacle could be...

- Your tie just won't tie right.
- You burnt the eggs and now you are upset that you didn't have a chance to eat before coming to church.
- Your car is acting up.
- Your spouse wants to argue before you walk out the door to hear a Word from the Lord.
- Your children are giving you attitudes before going to Worship.

Whatever your obstacle may be, you must go through it to get to Jesus.

The Bible reports that the men went through the roof to get to Jesus. The house was packed. They couldn't get through the front door. They couldn't get through the back door, so they went through the roof. Let's observe who's in attendance.

- The religious teachers are there.
- The Pharisees are there.
- The Galileans are there.
- The Judeans are there.
- The residents from Jerusalem are there.

There are all types of people surrounding this man that needs help.

> *That set the religion scholars and Pharisees buzzing. "Who does he think he is? That's blasphemous talk! God and only God can forgive sins."*

Jesus knew exactly what they were thinking and said, "Why all this gossipy whispering? Which is simpler: to say 'I forgive your sins,' or to say 'Get up and start walking'?

Well, just so it's clear that I'm the Son of Man and authorized to do either, or both..."

He now spoke directly to the paraplegic: "Get up. Take your bedroll and go home." Without a moment's hesitation, he did it—got up, took his blanket, and left for home, giving glory to God all the way. The people rubbed their eyes, incredulous—and then also gave glory to God. Awestruck, they said, "We've never seen anything like that!" (Luke 5:21-26 MSG)

It's amazing how we can see from the text, there were some foul witnesses surrounding this man. The text says that after this man received his healing, the Pharisees get upset with Jesus saying, "Who does He think He is? Only God can forgive sins." Don't be shocked, but you may have some foul witnesses in your life. The problem is they aren't like the Pharisees, they won't get mad at Jesus about your healing or your blessing, but they'll get mad and upset with you. However, you don't need to respond to foul witnesses. If they're not big enough to talk to God about what He's doing in your life, then they don't earn the right to talk to you. The next time somebody gets upset with you about the blessings of God on your life, you should tell them, "Don't hate the player, hate the game. I'm just happy to be blessed by God."

Not only did this man have some foul witnesses in his midst, but he also was surrounded by faith walkers. The Bible says after the man received his help and his healing, there were another group of people that glorified and praised God for his healing. You have one group hating your blessing and then you have another group happy for your blessing. One group despises your healing, but then you have another group that is dancing and praising God with you for your healing.

Which group of people are you listening to?

3 Steps Up

You now have an opportunity to begin to apply the truths from God's Word to your own situations. Take the time to go through this section before you move onto the next chapter which will take you deeper into how to take these steps. You have read about walking up the "3 Steps Up."

Step One: Look Up – Aware

What are some examples of times you were in need of help and help arrive?
Describe how you felt when you received this help?
Take the time to thank God for sending this help to you.

Step Two: Get Up – Arise–Move Forward One Step at a Time

Since you know how good it felt to receive help, who do you see around you that could use your help?
Who in your family could use your help?
Who in your neighborhood could use your help?
Who in your workplace could use your help?
Who in your church could use your help?
Step out and be an instrument God can use to help others in His name.

Step Three: Stay Up- Act – Stay Focused, Stay in the Good Fight, & Finish Strong

When you obey God, He will not give you more than you can handle. In fact, because you obeyed His voice and willingly helped others, your blessing is going to be so great you're going to have to share the overflow with those that are connected to you.

Review the passages from Luke 5:4-26 describing Jesus' ministry to others from this chapter and record what God reveals to you concerning stepping up out of your rut by helping others.

Meditate on and Memorize:

> *The thief comes only in order to steal and kill and destroy. I came that they may have and enjoy life, and have it in abundance [to the full, till it overflows].* (John 10:10 AMP)

Thank God for this promise from Jesus.

Chapter 3

Moving Up without Looking Back

"But disappointment always looks back
instead of looking up.
Looking up moves us up beyond where we are
to a new place of possibility and hope."[6]

In the last chapter, we discovered three important steps for moving up and forward.

1. **Look Up: Aware**
2. **Get Up: Arise–Move Forward One Step at a Time**
3. **Stay Up: Act – Stay Focused, Stay in the Good Fight, & Finish Strong**

Here's the thing: many people start the race of life but only a few stay focused, keep the faith, and finish strong. This may be the hardest chapter in the book for you to believe, receive, and stay moving up and forward.

Decide Now Not to Look Back, Go Back, or Turn Back

Your past does not determine your future. You cannot drive a car forward by constantly looking into your rearview mirror or in (today's era) your car's computer screen. It is impossible to be a new creation in Jesus Christ while holding onto the old things in your past. 2 Corinthians 5:17 reveals that when *any person is in Christ Jesus, that person is a new creation; the old things are passing away and all things are becoming new.*

If you find yourself stuck in the past, then getting unstuck can only happen when you focus on God's new thing, new future, and new possibilities. His plans for you is to give you hope and a future. God isn't into punishing you for your past; He's propelling you into your future which is filled with continual fresh starts and second chances.

Many of us are far beyond receiving a second chance. You wouldn't want anyone to know that you were on your hundredth chance, but never forget God is graceful and merciful in giving chances. The question for those that may judge your past on receiving chance after chance would be, "Where would they be if God didn't grant them chance after chance?" I've learned that people are fast to judge your past and slow to remember their own past failures and mistakes. If we can be honest with ourselves, it hurts when you're characterized or judged on your past. It can make you feel like a failure if you're continually looking back and not looking forward.

I can remember feeling like a failure as it related to my education growing up. I didn't really like school. Alright, I did say let's be honest. I despised school. My senior year of high school I got into trouble and had to settle for just a High School Diploma. I didn't have the honor and joy of walking across the stage and hearing my name called. This weighed on me as many would remind me of this moment in my life. To me, this felt like a failure because I kept looking back at this moment.

What I couldn't see was that God would provide other celebratory moments and milestones in my life. I couldn't see this because I kept looking back. It wasn't until I started looking forward and went from a High School diploma to an associate degree in Ministry. I kept looking forward and obtained my bachelor's degree in Christian Ministry. I kept looking forward and received my Master of Divinity degree. I kept on looking forward and worked hard and earned my Doctor of Ministry degree. I don't say this for any self-satisfaction because all honor is due to God. I simply say it to share the lesson with you that I have learned from this journey.

As long as I was looking back and remained idle in that situation of not moving, I had constant reminders. When I kept looking forward and had a spirit to receive all God had for me, the constant reminders were nowhere around. God showed me that there will always be people that will love to fish in your past but will fall away in the blessings of your present.

I say to you, no matter what condition or circumstance you may be in, keep looking forward and don't turn back.

So, I want you to make a new declaration this week.

"I will not turn back, look back, or go back.
I will seize every God-given new thing that
He has for me to think, feel, and do!"

Seize God's New with a Fresh Perspective

Putting on a pair of glasses will change your vision, focus, and perspective. A *perspective* is the way you look at people and things; perspective sees everything in a new light, a fresh take on how you think, feel, and react to something or someone. Remember that your perspective is often shaped or framed by your expectations.

Envision or imagine a picture of tomorrow's tasks, job, or work that you have. Now, frame that picture with the expectation that the day will be cloudy and stormy. No matter what's in the picture, the mood set by your perspective and expectation will be gloomy and depressing.

Now, frame tomorrow's picture with clear, bright, sunny skies. Not a cloud is in the sky and there is blue sky from horizon to horizon. No matter what's in that picture, the mood set by your perspective and expectation is hopeful and upbeat. Yes, your moving up, looking up, and going up instead of going back.

Consider Isaiah 43:19 where God declares:

"Behold, I will do a new thing,
 Now it shall spring forth;
 Shall you not know it?
 I will even make a road in the wilderness
 And rivers in the desert."

The Hebrew word for *new* is *chadash* which can also be translated "fresh." Take a moment, breathe in deeply and imagine yourself inhaling fresh air from a breeze blowing right after a plummeting rain shower. How refreshing and renewing that fresh air is. Or, breathe in deeply and imagine the smell of *your favorite dessert*. Ah...you begin salivating and hungering to taste a slice or piece right away. Or, imagine for a moment

21

the parched, dry taste in your mouth from being beaten down upon by a scorching sun in the desert. How you are thirsting for a cup of fresh, cold water from a palm-lined oasis.

Fresh certainly gives a different perspective to what might be old, moldy stale desert, stale air in a shut-up room, or salty, rank water drawn from a muddy ditch. Yes, God's future for you as you move up, go up, and look up is framed by His perspective. Remember, God said that His ways are not your ways nor His thoughts your thoughts.

I remember calling one of our members that was on the sick and shut-in list of our church. From past visits and observations, frailty and feebleness had already commenced to take its course. So, in my mind I already had the perspective of what to expect when I called. I was expecting a faint voice answering the phone. To my surprise, I was greeted with vibrancy and zeal. The new report was a shift had taken place and what was had been surpassed by the freshness of something new that had taken place. I called to encourage them, but before I got off the phone, they were encouraging me. You never know what God has for you. This was God's way of showing me how to change my perspective. Stop looking at the "what was" and start believing God for the "what is."

Let me help you understand one way that God is making you into a new creation and conforming you to the image and identity of Christ Jesus. Jesus teaches us that we cannot put new wine into old wineskins. New wine expands as it ferments. Old wineskins do not have the flexibility to stretch and accommodate the new wine. Likewise, when old, painful memories try to contain a new plan that God has for us, they distort the unfolding plan that what God intends to be new and fresh turns out painful just like the past. God is making you a new creation, a new wineskin, so you can receive and grow into the new ways God desires to work in and through you.

The next declaration I want you to make regularly and often is this:

◇◇◇

I refuse to let the past determine or frame my future.
I will joyfully and thankfully receive
God's new and fresh plans for my future.

◇◇◇

Move Up and NEVER Look Back

I am captivated by Paul's perspective on the new things God does in life...

> ...***Forgetting*** *those things which are behind and*
> ***Reaching forward*** *to those things which are ahead,*
> *I* ***press toward*** *the goal for the prize*
> *of the* ***upward*** *call of God in Christ Jesus.*
> (Philippians 3:13-14)

Go back for a moment with me to Isaiah 43:19. In this verse God announces that He is doing a new thing and we need a fresh perspective to see it. In the preceding verse, God tells us to do what Paul wrote that he was doing: "Do not remember the former things, nor consider the things of old." Wipe the slate clean. Take the eraser of your will and remove the old stuff on your memory's chalkboard. Do you remember the chalkboard in school? If, the teacher would try to write over the old notes on it without first erasing them, the teacher would be confusing the whole class. The teacher must wipe that board clean and then write a new message or note. Are you trying to just write over the past without erasing it completely? How is that working for you?

As we conclude these thoughts, I urge you to start constantly declaring this for yourself:

◇◇

I am not the prisoner of my past faults and failures.
I am forgiven...a new creation in Christ Jesus.
I will forget the past and
implement the good plans God has for me.

◇◇

Meditate on and Memorize:

Adapted from 2 Corinthians 5:17,

I am a new creation in Christ,

old things are passing away;

Behold, for me, all things are becoming new.

Write down an old hurt you will forget and a past person you will forgive:

_____

_____

_____

Chapter 4

Ask for What You Need

Transforming Your Trauma from Drama to Decisive Declaration

> "If you can't fly, then run, If you can't run, then walk, If you
> can't walk, then crawl, but whatever you do, you have to
> keep moving forward."–Martin Luther King Jr.[7]

You can change Post Traumatic Stress Syndrome into Post Traumatic Success Decisions (PTSD). To do this, you begin with asking and acting. Ask for what you need and take action to move out of your past hurts, pains, and offenses. Often a crisis in life will make you aware of just how stuck you are and give you an awareness of the need to ask and act. Let's explore together how to transform your trauma from drama to decisive declaration.

When Your Crisis Leads You to Christ

There has been a series of crises that have swept through the land such as unexpected fires breaking out, the gusting of tornadoes and hurricanes, riots, murders, sex trafficking, and continual reports of abuse and betrayal in families. One of the most traumatic crises this nation is experiencing now is the uprising of the law enforcement being accused of killing African Americans. This outcry from the urban community has highlighted the extreme injustices that many endure based on their skin color and not the content of their character. In fact, researchers have suggested that people of color in general were found more likely to be killed by police than their white counterparts.

Even with this information many will compose their own opinion on how justice should be served. In my own conclusion of enduring fair justice, I remember reading a story of an African American male that was mentally ill and had to be restrained by being bound by a rope and tied to a horse while a police officer displayed his authority while walking through the streets of Galveston County, Texas. As cruel and harsh as that may seem, that's just one of many debates among the African American Community.

Another debate that happened was the response of a young man who was the brother of deceased Botham Jean showing empathy to his brothers' killer. For those of you who aren't familiar with the story let me bring you abreast to what transpired. It was a Caucasian female Officer by the name of Amber Guyger who walked into the apartment of Botham Jean who was African American and shot him dead. Her explanation for this killing was she thought she was in her apartment only to find out she walked into his apartment. After going to trial, she was convicted of murder and sentenced to ten years in prison. Brandt Jean asked the judge, "Can I hug her and let her know I forgive her for her actions?"

The young man said, "My main desire isn't for you to go to jail, but to give your life to Christ." This statement shocked the nation so much that every news outlet including MSNBC had to talk about Christ. They had to agree that act of forgiveness exemplifies what Jesus would do in a situation like this. This suggests God will allow crisis situations to arise in our lives to display the character of Jesus Christ.

◇◇◇

**The Jean brothers' mother said,
"Regardless of the views of spectators, walk with God always.
Forgiveness is for the forgiver and
it doesn't matter what the forgiven does with it."**

◇◇◇

People may talk about you, lie about you, and scandalize your name, but when you know who you are and whose you are you can forgive them because you understand what God has done for you. Remember,

- Don't waste your time worrying about how others respond to your forgiveness.
- Refuse to be upset when others do not say they are sorry.
- Reject feelings of frustration when people lie to you or about you.
- Don't get bent out of shape because others did not put on Social Media how appreciative they were for your acts of kindness or affirming words.

One of the most misinterpreted understandings is believing that forgiving others makes you weak. Please hear my heart when you read this and put this in your spirit, "When you forgive, it doesn't make you weak." When you forgive, you're just releasing dead weight that has the ability to hold you back from the blessings of God. Holding on to offense and unforgiveness hurts and hinders you. Let's be very clear forgiving isn't an easy assignment. Forgiving was one of the life lessons that I had to learn. I had to understand that forgiving others would help me rather than hinder me.

The reason this was difficult for me to do in the beginning was because I just couldn't comprehend showing compassion and love to those who simply hurt me. To me I wanted the other party to know that I was angry, upset and bitter. I didn't want to have any dealings with them because I felt that my trust, loyalty and respect had been violated. But when you come to the realization that your forgiveness is not only for the person, but to also release you from the bondage of always living in that broken moment. It took some time for me to grasp this life lesson, but when I did comprehend this, I started my journey of being free.

Years ago, I heard a simple formula for repentance which Bishop T.D. Jakes preached about:

- *Admit it.* Admit that you are hurt, offended, and angry. Go to God and repent. Ask His forgiveness. Receiving His forgiveness and mercy empowers us to be merciful and forgiving of others.
- *Quit it.* Release it. Stop doing what's wrong. Just do the right thing. Love instead of hate. Forgive instead of holding onto unforgiveness and offense. Bless others instead of cursing them.
- *Forget it.* Stop rehearsing the past. Don't go fishing in the past and continually bringing up your mistakes or the failures of others. Corrie ten Boom admits when she thought about what her enemies had done to her:

"Even as the angry vengeful thoughts boiled through me, I saw the sin of them. Jesus Christ had died for this man; was I going to ask for more? Lord Jesus, I prayed, forgive me and help me to forgive him... Jesus, I cannot forgive him. Give me your forgiveness... And so I discovered that it is not on our forgiveness any more than on our goodness that the world's healing hinges, but on his. When he tells us to love our enemies, he gives along with the command, the love itself."

"God takes our sins – the past, present, and future, and
dumps them in the sea and puts up a sign that says NO
FISHING ALLOWED."[8]

Repentance and forgiveness go hand in hand in getting us unstuck.
How so? When someone intentionally or unintentionally hurts us, we
must move beyond our pain and refuse to take up the bait of Satan which
is offense. When hurt, we have to choose between two options—offense
or forgiveness. Likewise, when we hurt another person, we have two
options—staying offended or admitting our offense and repenting of it.

When you admit you have sinned against God or another person, you
have repented. To repent means to turn away from a hurt, offense, sin
or transgression and turn to God and ask forgiveness. Walking in the
forgiving love of God's light, also allows us to forgive others. Jesus says
about the prostitute who anoints his feet with oil, "I tell you, her sins—
and they are many—have been forgiven, so she has shown me much love.
But a person who is forgiven little shows only little love" (Luke 7:47-48
NIV). God has been infinitely merciful, forgiving, and loving of you. Do
the same toward others—forgive them, extend grace to them, be merciful
and love them.

I encourage you to say, "I didn't do it for them, but I'm doing this
for me. I forgive my Father; this is for me. I forgive my Mother; this is
for me. I forgive my brothers and my sisters; this is for me. I forgive my
co-workers. I forgive the disgruntled church folk that laugh in my face
and talk behind my back."

Stuck in a Crisis?

The Gospels tell us about a woman who comes to Jesus. She is in crisis
mode. Mark chapter 5 illuminates her critical situation. He tells us about

a woman that has a crisis that she could longer handle herself. Matthew, Mark, and Luke tell the same story about this woman, but they simply don't mention her name. Matthew, Mark, and Luke are the Synoptic Gospels which simply means, "The Same." They tell the same story from a different perspective.

But why do Matthew and Mark withhold this women's identity? I concluded her name isn't mentioned because we would be too focused on who she was instead of who she's connected to. The problem in the era we live now is too many people want to know who failed, who didn't make it, and who messed up instead of trying to see how they made it out and how they overcame the hand of the enemy. You should not be concerned about my name, your concern should be how did I survive.

I really believe they didn't mention her name because where she's nameless we can insert our name right there. Instead of saying, "A woman had issues," just put your name in her place. Not a woman with an issue, but Jesse with an issue. John with an issue. William with an issue. Tina with an issue. The reason her name isn't important is because all of us have issues that we don't want our name attached to. The God we serve is bigger than the issue that has you nameless! Don't be embarrassed about your issue because your issue is bringing you closer to Christ.

What brings this woman to Christ? The first thing that brings her to Christ is her description. Mark 5:25 says, "A woman who had suffered a condition." This woman is described as a suffering individual. Too often, we get upset about how we are described by other people. What you don't understand is how they describe you is an indication on how He is going to bless you. You can't survive without suffering. You can't be healed without being sick. You can't be brought out without being in. You can't be touched without being stepped on. You can't be lifted up without being down.

◇◇
**Whatever and however others describe
your present circumstance and situation,
your response should be, "It's leading me closer to Christ."**
◇◇

Your reality can be this...

- I'm hurt, but I'm getting closer.
- I'm confused and frustrated, but I'm getting closer.
- I'm down and out, but I'm getting closer to Christ.

Paul wrote, "We are hard-pressed on every side, yet not crushed; we are perplexed, but not in despair; persecuted, but not forsaken; struck down, but not destroyed" (2 Corinthians 4:8-9 NIV). Make a daily declaration, "My crisis didn't destroy me, it just led me to His hands. It led me to His heart. My crisis is just leading me to Christ." This woman's description led her to Christ.

Not only did her description lead her to Christ, but her determination led her to Christ. The Bible says this woman had been bleeding for twelve years and after her doctors took all her money, her condition grew worse, but she hears about Jesus (see Mark 5:26-27). This woman had lived as an outcast for twelve long years. You have to understand that she was deemed as being uncleaned and couldn't be engage or embraced by people. She didn't have any friends to help her. She didn't have any family to help her and the ones that were qualified to help made things even more difficult for her. This is to suggest to us that although they have the title and credentials, that doesn't qualify them to know your crisis.

You get so caught up in wanting to be connected to things that you think can help you and you rush into ungodly connections because you're operating off of your desires and not your discernment. You put your crisis on Social Media looking for likes and views and you're still in the same crisis. Stop waiting until you spend everything you have and discover what

31

Christ can do. If you open up your mouth and declare His Word as a sign of determination, God will show you how to take care of the issue.

It was her description, her determination, and also her deliverance that led her to Christ. Don't miss it. Most people think her touching Jesus' garment was the deliverance of the text. The Deliverance of the text is in verse 28 when the Bible says, "She thought to herself, if I can just touch His clothes I can get well." In other words, she talked to herself. Sometimes, you have to have a "Me, Myself, and I" moment and encourage yourself.

In my first book, "No More Distractions," I have a chapter entitled, "The Me, Myself and I Distraction." The truth is you have to have moments of solitude. When people walk off and leave you, be your own cheering squad. You have to be like David and encourage yourself in the Lord.

"God does not give us everything we want,
but He does fulfill His promises,
leading us along the best and straightest paths to Himself."
- Dietrich Bonhoeffer[9]

These women through their actions were asking God for what they needed. They were moving from the drama of their trauma to decisive declaration through their words and actions.

Are you stuck in the past which is filled with the pain and hurt of what others have done to you or you have done to yourself? Get unstuck. Repent. Forgive. Pray. Ask God for what you need...not for what you want.

We cannot change or blame others. Only when we take responsibility for what we can do, will we be able to move from crisis to creative, positive solutions. I invite you to make these positive declarations:
- *I will forgive even before he/she repents.*
- *I refuse to take up an offense.*

- *God has forgiven me; I will forgive others.*
- *I refuse to go back to the past. My past does not determine my future.*
- *I cannot change others, but I can change me.*

Moments of Release

You now have an opportunity to begin to apply the truths from God's Word to your own situations. Take the time to go through this section. You have now learned your words, your determination, and your decision to declare God's promises which brings resolution to your issues.

What issues are you facing?

Find a promise in God's Word that tells you God's solution to each issue.

Record in a journal what God does and then be prepared to share your testimony to those God sends across your path.

Chapter 5

The Rules of Repentance

Repentance: The Key Opening the Door to Transformation

> *From that time Jesus began to preach, crying out, "Repent* ***(change your mind for the better, heartily amend your ways, with abhorrence of your past sins),*** *for the kingdom of heaven is at hand."* (Matthew 4:17 AMP emphasis added)

Repent means to change your mind for the better and amend your ways. In order to repent, you must have abhorrence (hate, disgust, revulsion) for your past sins. Jesus is warning His listeners that this is a necessary step in preparation for the arrival of the kingdom of heaven.

> *And Peter answered them, Repent* ***(change your views and purpose to accept the will of God in your inner selves instead of rejecting it)*** *and be baptized, every one of you, in the name of Jesus Christ for the forgiveness of and release*

from your sins; and you shall receive the gift of the Holy Spirit. (Acts 2:38 AMP emphasis added)

Peter adds that repentance includes changing your views and purpose so they match the will of God. This is to be done willingly. Peter inferred this was necessary to receive forgiveness of and release from your sins.

7 Marks of Repentance

Godly sorrow brings repentance that leads to salvation and leaves no regret, but worldly sorrow brings death. **See what this godly sorrow has produced in you: what earnestness, what eagerness to clear yourselves, what indignation, what alarm, what longing, what concern, what readiness to see justice done. At every point you have proved yourselves to be innocent in this matter.** (2 Corinthians 7:10-12 NIV emphasis added)

#1 – Earnestness

- *Being eager to clear myself with God.* Repentance and confession is not a ritual. It's not about feeling better. I must rush back to my First love, Jesus Christ. I am remorsefully sincere about getting right with God. My sin created a distance, a gap, a separation between me and the Lover of my soul. He didn't move; I did. I must rush back to Him!
- *Running to earnestly repent (at the altar).* The altar is both physical and spiritual. We are to confess our sins to one another. We publicly confess Christ as our only Savior and Lord. I may be too proud to repent before others. I need to "get over it." Both the altar

of the church, or in front of my family or friends, and at the altar of my heart. In liturgical communions like Anglican, Catholic, and Eastern Orthodox, the sacrament (i.e. sacred moment) of Confession is always public before priest and saints. I must set aside my pride and mask of goodness to run to the altar.

- *Weeping earnest tears of sorrow.* We read about weeping tears of sorrow throughout the Scriptures and the history of the Church. Such earnest, tearful repentance is graphically described in Joel:

"Now, therefore," says the Lord,
"Turn to Me with all your heart,
With fasting, with weeping, and with mourning."
So rend your heart, and not your garments;
Return to the Lord your God,
For He is gracious and merciful,
Slow to anger, and of great kindness;
And He relents from doing harm.
Who knows if He will turn and relent,
And leave a blessing behind Him —
A grain offering and a drink offering
For the Lord your God?
(Joel 2:12-14)

- *Repenting not because I am caught but eager to change.* The familiar adage is "Admit it; Quit it; Forget it." Repentance isn't real unless there is change in heart, attitude, and actions. Stop going to the altar again and again to repent of the same addiction, abuse, or action that is hurtful. Quit it! Change!

#2 – Eagerness to Clear Myself

- *Cleared of excess baggage.* Burn your baggage from the past. Let go of the restraints that have kept you stuck. Say, "I must clear myself of all burdensome sin!"

- *Eager to be clean.* After sweating playing basketball or exercising, I am ready for a cleansing, soapy shower that will wash away the dirt and grim. Likewise, I am eager to be cleansed of the stain of sin through repentance.

- *Ready to not give the devil or sin a foothold in my life.* My grasp on anything worldly must be released. Am I ready to let go and let God have full control of my thoughts, feelings, and actions?

- *Eager to not be on the defensive.* Remember one of A.W. Tozer's "Five Spiritual Vows" is *never defend yourself.* God is our sure defense. I must stop making excuses, fighting back, and refusing to turn the other cheek. It's time to lower my defenses and hide myself in the everlasting arms of the Father.

- *Eager to be bold for Christ and never ashamed.* A preeminent mark of the early apostles in Acts was boldness. I must refuse to whisper my faith; I must boldly proclaim that Jesus has forgiven my sins, healed my brokenness, and made me whole. The outcome of repentance and being forgiven is boldness: "And they [the early Christians] were all filled with the Holy Spirit, and they spoke the word of God with boldness" (Acts 4:31).

#3–Indignation

- *Disgusted with myself.* Ever heard someone say, "Don't beat yourself up over that." Really? My sins, works of the flesh, and transgressions, wickedness and iniquity, either intentional or unintentional, should disgust me. My sin isn't a pretty picture no matter how

I try to spin it. Get over yourself, be disgusted...real shame and guilt do lead to self-indignation and repentance. The Jews of old would publicly sit in an ash heap, tear their clothes, and cry out with disgust, sorrow, and indignation over their sin.

- *Desire to crucify the flesh.* Flesh as used by Paul in writing about the works of the flesh (read Galatians 5) is our sin nature. We are pre-disposed to sin. It's called "original sin" (read Psalm 51). When we consciously refuse to sin and do what's right, we crucify the flesh. I must refuse to follow my instincts and say, feel or do whatever wrong jumps out of me. I must be quick to listen, slow to speak, and slow to anger (James 1:19).

- *Holy revulsion.* My sin revulsed me. To be revulsed is to move back from, turn away from something odious. My sin revulsed me just like the smell of sour milk or vomit.

- *Indignant nausea – I want to throw up – To vomit the toxin or poison from my being.* Food poisoning or ingesting something toxic makes us want to puke. So must our sin. Such indignation drives us to repent.

#4–Alarm

- *Fear of God.* Proverbs teaches us that fearing God is the beginning of all wisdom, knowledge, and understanding. Yes, to fear God is to stand in awe of Him but it also means trepidation. I am so alarmed by the consequences of my sin, that I repent. Yes, Jesus died on the cross to take my sins away, but my continual sinning makes His grace cheap. I should be alarmed by my frivolous attitude toward God. I find myself, at times, fearing man more than God. My fear of God produces an alarm in me before I sin, keeping me in the position of repenting even of the desires and passions I feel before I act upon them. Do you have an alarm that sounds within your conscience before you sin? Failing to fear God is simply contempt for Him.

- *Alarmed by the deceitfulness of sin.* Believing Satan's lies instead of being alarmed by them leads us to sin and destruction. Deception is all around us. Atrocious news distracts us from believing the Good News. Counterfeit faith and cheap grace abound around and within us. Consider this powerful text from 1 Timothy 1:5-7 (MSG), "The whole point of what we're urging is simply love — love uncontaminated by self-interest and counterfeit faith, a life open to God. Those who fail to keep to this point soon wander off into cul-de-sacs of gossip. They set themselves up as experts on religious issues but haven't the remotest idea of what they're holding forth with such imposing eloquence." Don't be deceive by religious or spiritual talk that sounds good or profound. The simple truth of the Gospel is often undermined by subtle lies that pollutes and deceives us. Be alarmed...if it sounds too good to be true...it's most likely a lie and you should be alarmed.
- *Lying to or conning myself.* If you continually take your own advice, you may be believing a fool. Proverbs 12:15 teaches, "The way of a fool is right in his own eyes, But he who heeds counsel is wise." Surround yourself with godly saints who not only know what's right, they practice righteousness.
- *Fearing spiritual blindness.* Conspiracy theories are not an invention of the Internet. They started in the Garden with the deception of the Serpent. Whenever the alarm of your conscience goes off when sparked by the conviction of the Holy Spirit who teaches and guides you in all truth, then you must stop, look both ways,

and listen to the truth instead of blinding setting foot into a broad highway of destruction.

- *Alarmed that my lack of vigilance to repent has kept me from loving God totally.* Watch out all the time. Prepare yourself with the armor of God to face spiritual attacks from all sides and at all times. Be vigilant and know the wiles of the Devil. Avoid quick and snap decisions. Vigilance requires that you do due diligence with the Word, Wise Counsel, and allowing the Spirit of God to Work in and through you.

#5–Longing

Once you rebuke Satan, Sin, Worldliness, ***What will be your longing? Your pursuit?***

- *Pursue God.* A.W. Tozer in *The Pursuit of God,* writes…
  "O God, I have tasted Thy goodness, and it has both satisfied me and made me thirsty for more. I am painfully conscious of my need for further grace. I am ashamed of my lack of desire. O God, the Triune God, I want to want Thee; I long to be filled with longing; I thirst to be made more thirsty still. Show me Thy glory, I pray Thee, so that I may know Thee indeed. Begin in mercy a new work of love within me. Say to my soul, 'Rise up my love, my fair one, and come away.' Then give me grace to rise and follow Thee up from this misty lowland where I have wandered so long."[10]
- *Pursue holiness and purity.* Dr. Larry Keefauver has quipped that what Christian leaders need the most are, "The fear of God, holiness, and humility."[11] Those who pursue and long for these traits are leaders worth following. Are you such a leader?

- *Long for childlike innocence.* Our culture confuses innocence with naivety. We think that faith is complicated and refuse to embrace the discipline of simplicity. Too often, we long for what's puffed up and overstated instead of the simple truth. Jesus bids us to come to him as little children. Can I return to a childlike, simple and innocent faith without guile?
- *Longing for His Presence.* Are your days filled with a longing for Heaven and for Him? Can you see yourself as a new creation in Christ, becoming a child again, refusing to be distracted by pharisaic intellectualism and legalism, and pursuing what's godly and pure?

#6 – Concern (Zeal)

- *Zeal for Christ.* When have you last heard the word "zeal" describe a believer in Christ? Oh, I hear the word describe sports fans and politicians, but rarely Christians. In fact, the word "zealot" has come to denote something negative in our vocabulary, like a "religious zealot" referring most often to a terrorist or fundamentalist. So, the contemporary Christian martyrs in Syria, Iran, Egypt, Nigeria, and China, are they not zealots? Should we not have such zeal for Christ?
- *Fanatical desire to please God.* Oh my, there's another socially and politically unacceptable words today—*fanatic*. Too often, I find myself more concerned with pleasing man than pleasing God. After all, I don't want to be fired from my job, divorced from my spouse, disowned by my children, or disfellowshipped by my church for not pleasing some, right? Really? Yes, concern and passionate zeal are not in vogue...but they are in Scripture.

- *Passionately in love with God.* The Greek word for passion means "to die." Such is understood when we say, "The Passion of Christ."
- *Rushing to restore the relationship.* About someone who is a backslider, we remark that *he is running from God.* About a repentant believer, we should say, *he is rushing and running toward God.* I must constantly run the race towards Jesus Christ!
- *Can't live without Him!* Longing for God means that I constantly choose to walk in the Light not in the dark. I continually live for Him instead of living for myself. I cannot think, feel, or do anything that would bring disgrace of shame to the glory of God in Christ. I can't live a moment without Him.

#7 – Readiness to see justice done
- *Avenging of Wrong (as translated in the KJV).* Repentance may well require that I do something more than repent to God. I want to act justly to restore and reconcile in any situation where I harmed, hurt, or caused loss in a situation.
- *Restitution.* If I need to repay a person for a financial loss, restore and reconcile in a fair way, or personally repent to that person, then I am willing to do what's right without causing any further harm or hurt to that person.
- *I have wronged you; I want to make it right.* If God and godly counselors agree in guiding me to do the right things, then I will make every effort to do what's right.
- *Paying my debts and my vows.* It may take months or years to repay a debt, but we must be willing to restore whatever is within our ability to do so.

Sanctification = Transformation

*"...elect according to the foreknowledge of God the Father, in **sanctification** of the Spirit, for obedience and sprinkling of the blood of Jesus Christ."* (1 Peter 1:2 NKJV emphasis added)

*"Now may the God of peace Himself **sanctify** you completely; and may your whole spirit, soul, and body be preserved blameless at the coming of our Lord Jesus Christ. **He who calls you is faithful, who also will do it."** (1 Thessalonians 5:23-24 NKJV emphasis added)*

And may the God of peace Himself sanctify you through and through [separate you from profane things, make you pure and wholly consecrated to God]; and may your spirit and soul and body be preserved sound and complete [and found] blameless at the coming of our Lord Jesus Christ (the Messiah). Faithful is He Who is calling you [to Himself] and utterly trustworthy, and He will also do it [fulfill His call by hallowing and keeping you]. (1 Thessalonians 5:23-24 AMPC emphasis added)

Transformation = Offering ourselves as living sacrifices; being transformed by the renewing of one's mind—*nous* (Romans 12:1-2).

Therefore I urge you, brothers and sisters, by the mercies of God, to present your bodies [dedicating all of yourselves, set apart] as a living sacrifice, holy and well-pleasing to God,

*which is your rational (logical, intelligent) act of worship.
And do not be conformed to this world [any longer with
its superficial values and customs], but be transformed and
progressively changed [as you mature spiritually] by the
renewing of your mind [focusing on godly values and ethical
attitudes], so that you may prove [for yourselves] what the
will of God is, that which is good and acceptable and perfect
[in His plan and purpose for you].* (AMP emphasis added)

Transformed, from the Greek word meaning "metamorphosis," refers
to the process that leads to an outward, permanent change. Verse two
indicates this a progressive change as you mature spiritually. This change
is accomplished by the renewing of your mind by focusing on godly
values and ethical attitudes instead of those presented by worldly cus-
toms and values.

Ethics is the study of good and evil, right and wrong. Godly ethics are
grounded in the character of God. Bonhoeffer asks, "Who stands fast?
Only the man whose final standard is not his reason, his principles, his
conscience, his freedom, or his virtue, but who is ready to sacrifice all
this when he is called to obedient and responsible action in faith and in
exclusive allegiance to God—the responsible man, who tries to make his
whole life an answer to the question and call of God. Where are these
responsible people?"[12]

Worldly values can include wealth, power, pleasure, revenge, fame,
vanity, and status and promote jealousies, resentments, and conflicts
among people. The values taught in the Bible are often the opposite of
worldly values: kindness and respect for all people instead of power;
humility instead of status; honesty and generosity instead of wealth;
self-control instead of self-indulgence; forgiveness instead of revenge.

Christian values promote peace and good will among people in accordance with the purposes of God.[13]

Examine Yourself

> *So anyone who eats this bread or drinks this cup of the Lord unworthily is guilty of sinning against* **the body and blood of the Lord. That is why you should examine yourself before eating the bread and drinking the cup. For if you eat the bread or drink the cup without honoring the body of Christ, you are eating and drinking God's judgment upon yourself. That is why many of you are weak and sick and some have even died.** (1 Corinthians 11:27 emphasis added)

Repent and Get Over It: Move beyond your past hurts, sins, failures, pain, fears, uncertainties, doubts, and mistakes. Then, turn away from your wrong and sinful habits. Turn to Jesus Christ and ask forgiveness (1 John 1:9). Finally, start following Jesus (Matthew 16:24) in word and deed.

⋄⋄

The Divine Process and Work of the Spirit in Us is Sanctification.

⋄⋄

This Is God's End Game for You

> *For those whom He foreknew [and loved and chose beforehand], He also predestined to be conformed to the image of His Son [and ultimately share in His complete sanctification],*

so that He would be the firstborn [the most beloved and hon-ored] among many believers. (Romans 8:29 AMP)

God's will is that we be *telos—be perfect* even as our Father in heaven is perfect." God's will (desire, destiny) for us is to be "conformed to the image of Christ Jesus" which is to be "like Him."

Fragmentation is caused by original sin. It is separation from God and tore you away from the image of God and shattered your God-image into a broken, sin-infected self-image.

Transformation comes through repentance and turning to Jesus for the forgiveness of sin.

> *"That no flesh should glory in His presence.* **But of Him you are in Christ Jesus, who became for us wisdom from God — and righteousness and sanctification and redemption — that, as it is written, "He who glories, let him glory in the Lord."** (1 Corinthians 1:29-31 NKJV emphasis added)

> *"For this is the will of God, your* **sanctification."** (1 Thessalonians 4:3 NKJV emphasis added)

Sanctification is to be holy as God is holy. Our goal is to continually become more and more like Christ, the *Holy and Anointed One.*

> *That each of you should know how to possess his own vessel in* **sanctification** *and honor,* **not in passion of lust, like the Gentiles who do not know God.** (1 Thessalonians 4:4-6 NKJV emphasis added)

God from the beginning chose you for salvation through **sanctification** *by the Spirit and belief in the truth.* (2 Thessalonians 2:13 NKJV)

How Does Transformation Happen?

Therefore, since we have been justified through faith, we **have peace with God through our Lord Jesus Christ, through whom we have gained access by faith into this grace in which we now stand. And we rejoice in the hope of the glory of God. Not only so, but we also rejoice in our sufferings, because we know that suffering produces perseverance; perseverance, character; and character, hope. And hope does not disappoint us, because God has poured out his love into our hearts by the Holy Spirit, whom he has given us.** (Romans 5:1-5 NKJV emphasis added)

After repentance, the work of the Holy Spirit within us to change us moves us through a process of moving through and beyond our suffering/trials/tribulations to developing a patient, persevering character. As we move forward and mature, growing in our faith, we experience hope through the Spirit who continually manifests God's forgiving love. Whether we win or lose, fail or succeed, fall or overcome, God keeps empowering us toward victory in every circumstance. The only way we can fail ultimately is if we quit.

Character/Identity = Image and Likeness of Christ

> *And as we have borne the **image** of the man of dust, we shall also bear **the image of the heavenly Man.*** (1 Corinthians 15:49 NKJV emphasis added)

> *And we, who with unveiled faces all reflect **the Lord's glory, are being transformed into his likeness with ever-increasing glory, which comes from the Lord, who is the Spirit.*** (2 Corinthians 3:18 emphasis added)

Now we are ready to move to the next step in becoming like Christ. Repentance opens the door to God's power in the Holy Spirit to moving forward.

Chapter 6

The Relief of Moving On

Starting Today, I Need to Forget What's Gone, Appreciate What Remains, and Look Forward to What's Coming

Moving on and seeking the will of God can be difficult. This chapter will give understanding and highlight how to embrace change and move on.

> *Do not remember the former things,*
> *Nor consider the things of old.*
> *Behold, I will do a new thing,*
> *Now it shall spring forth;*
> *Shall you not know it?*
> *I will even make a road in the wilderness*
> *And rivers in the desert.*
> (Isaiah 43:18-19 NKJV)

I remember taking my family to a basketball game in Philadelphia, PA to the Wells Fargo Center to see Lebron James play. After the game, I had a conversation with my son about who was the greatest basketball player. At that time, Kobe Bryant wasn't close to retirement, but his game wasn't as vibrant as his youthful days. I told my son that Kobe Bryant is and always will be the greatest basketball player, in my opinion. I kept talking about how Kobe Bryant did this and how Kobe Bryant did that. At the time, Lebron James was the face for the NBA and this was my son's all-time favorite basketball player.

After listening to me for a while, my son said something to me that relates to the verses in Isaiah 43. "Dad you keep talking about what Kobe did in the past tense, but what is he doing now?"

At that moment, I caught myself living in the past and talking about the past, but couldn't speak on anything that Kobe was doing currently. That's what the prophet speaks about in the first couple of verses as it relates to simply getting over the past.

I had to come to the realization that although Kobe Bryant is and was great, Lebron James was the new thing. I was making the past my dwelling place. I didn't let my son win the debate on who is the greatest at the moment, but he did enlighten me on how living in the past can keep you stuck and stagnated. Here are some guided points to assist you in moving on from the past.

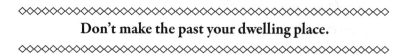

Don't make the past your dwelling place.

3 R's for handling the Past...

Rejoice in what God did. You have a choice when you sift through your memories. You can retain the bad ones or release them. You may also repeat them or learn from them. What will you choose?

Repent for the wrong you did. In the last chapter, we unpacked all the aspect of repentance. Remember that you can admit it—confess what you did wrong. Quit it—stop doing what's wrong and start doing what's right. And then, Forget It—release the past...learn from it but don't go back there.

Release the hurts inflicted by others. Refuse to be offended. Never take the bait of Satan—offense. In the Bait of Satan, John Brevere writes, "Offended people still may experience miracles, words of utterance, strong preaching, and healing in their lives. But these are gifts of the Spirit, not fruits. We will be judged according to fruit, not gifting. A gift is given. Fruit is cultivated."[14]

As the forgiving love of God in Christ transforms you into His image, you begin to manifest in your character, the fruit of the Holy Spirit. The gifts of the Spirit (1 Cor. 12) are the ministry of Christ through you; the fruit of the Spirit are the character of Christ in you. When you operate in the fruit of the Spirit, you became a servant as Jesus was (Philippians 2).

You Can Get Over It!

- **Get over the hurts inflicted by others because they are dead!**

  "For He is not the God of the dead but of the living, for all live to Him" (Luke 20:38).

- **Get over what you did wrong because it is forgiven!**

  "If we confess our sins, He is faithful and just to forgive us our sins and cleanse us from all unrighteousness" (1 John 1:9).

- **Get over what you may have had or lost in the past because the best is yet to come!**

"Now to Him who is able to do exceedingly abundantly above all that we ask or think, according to the power that works in us" (Ephesians 3:20-21).

Who is God and What is God doing?

◇◇◇
God is at work in you, around you and Right Now!
◇◇◇

1. **God is the God of the NOW...**
- He is the "I am." He was, is, and always will be.

> *"**Behold**, I will do a new thing,*
> *Now it shall spring forth;*
> *Shall you not know it?"*

Behold means:
- Get a grip and determine to move forward NOW!
- Open your eyes to what God is doing NOW!
- Listen carefully to what the Word of God is saying to you NOW!

He is the "I Am" which means He is present here and now. He is an up close and personal God.

He is Adonai, Lord!

Of every word that is spoken **now**...

Of every action that is done **now**...

Of every feeling, thought, and decision being made **now**...

God of the **Now** means no procrastination. It means saying, Yes, Lord and never saying, No, Lord.

2. God is the God of the NEW!

> *"Behold, I will do a **new** thing,*
> *Now it shall spring forth;*
> *Shall you not know it?"*

He is God of the Resurrection (John 10).

New means that we must...

- *Change* (2 Corinthians 3:17-18, 5:17). What has been comfortable gets tossed out the window. Everything will be new, different, and changed including us!
- *Fresh* (Psalm 92:10-15). Imagine the smell and taste of fresh bread versus the yuck of stale bread. Breathe in deeply the air in a well ventilated, breezy room versus the choking stench of a stale, shut up for weeks room. Taste refreshing fresh water versus the fowl taste of dirty water.
- *Completely*...All (Revelation 21:5). Change must be total, complete, pervasive for something or someone to be new.

New is *chadas*. To do a new thing is to renew, rebuild, and refresh. Examine each of these scriptures and see all the different things God wants to renew.

- 1 Samuel 11:4 – Renew the kingdom. Renew the kingdom of your world and the world around you.
- 2 Chronicles 15:8 – Renew the altar and house. God wants continually renewal of your worship at home and at church.

- Psalm 51:1 – Renew a right spirit. Anything wrong in your spirit needs to be washed away by the sanctifying flood of the Holy Spirit.
- Psalm 103:5 – Renew your youth like an eagle. Old ideas, traditions, thoughts, feelings, and behavior that do not honor and glorify God must die. You become a new creation in Christ.
- Psalm 104:30 – Renew the face of the earth. God wants you to care for and renew the earth.
- Isaiah 61:4 – Repair the waste cities and the desolations of generations. Every generational curse is broken; His blessings and mercies are new every morning for you and your family.
- Lamentations 5:21 – Renew our days. "From this day forward..." Each day is new, fresh, and filled with joy, hope, and thanksgiving. *This is the day the Lord has made and I will rejoice and be glad in it*, is your declaration.

The God of the New requires us to:
- *Get over the past!*
- *Get a grip on Him!*
- *Get into the new thing!*

◇◇

**Stop standing on the sidelines and get into the game!
In order to go on, you must get up!**

◇◇

God of the New demands we:
- Stop sitting around complaining. Start giving thanks.
- Stop standing around observing. Start getting involved.

- Stop looking around for someone else to do something you should be doing. Start getting God's work done.
- Stop waiting around for another train to come. Catch God's train to glory.

3. **God is the God of the Next**

   Get up...Get going...Get involved...
   Get on this glory train!
   God of the NEXT!

"Behold, I will do a new thing,
Now it shall spring forth;
Shall you not know it?
I will even make a road in the wilderness
And rivers in the desert."
(Isaiah 43:19 NKJV)

The Living God is God of the...
- **NEXT plan. Not your plan...His plan.**
- **NEXT step. Not your journey...His journey for you.**
- **NEXT direction. Not going your way...Going His Way!**
  - Jesus is the Alpha and Omega.
  - Christ is the Way, the truth, and the Life.
  - What He starts, He finishes (Philippians 1:6).
  - Are you willing to trust God your Father, Jesus your Savior and Lord, and The Holy Spirit your Comforter and Guide with what's next?

What if...

- **The next thing that God does in your life is the exact opposite of the last thing...**
  - ○ Like Jonah (chapter 4). Jonah probably hated the Assyrians for their cruel treatment of the Israelites. When God commanded him to go to their capital of Nineveh, Jonah went the opposite direction. God reversed his journey and put him on a journey directly to Nineveh. Instead of seeing God destroy the enemy, Jonah's preach brought repentance and salvation to the Assyrians.
  - ○ Like Abraham. Abraham and Sarah were old and childless. God promised them a baby in their old age through whom a mighty nation would arise for generations to come. So, Sarah gave birth to the promised baby, Isaac. As Isaac grew older, God then commanded Abraham to take him to a sacred mount or high place and sacrifice this promised child. Really? Obediently Abraham did just that and as he was about to sacrifice Isaac, God told him not to kill Isaac. Have a baby...kill the baby...don't kill the baby. Really?
  - ○ Like Mary. Virgin Mary was engaged to Joseph to be married. Then, God told her she would have a baby without any sexual intercourse with Joseph before the wedding. God then told Joseph the same thing and to marry his fiancé despite the social shame and reproach it might bring on them. Talk about reversing this couple's plans for life. Really?

So, if the next thing God asks you to do is the exact opposite of the last thing he required of you, would you still trust and obey Him?

The God of the NEXT requires:

- **Get on with it!** What does that mean?
  - Means getting up!
  - Means getting going!
  - Means getting involved!
- **Get moving on!**
  - Moving on can be Uncomfortable.
  - Moving on is dealing with the Unfamiliar.
  - Moving on is overcoming what you were formerly Unable to do.

Our God is God of the **Now, New, Next!**

And God is able to make all grace abound toward you [NOW], that you, always having all sufficiency in all things [NEW], may have an abundance for every good work [NEXT]. (2 Corinthians 9:8)

Moments of Release

You now have an opportunity to begin to apply the truths from God's Word presented in this powerful chapter to your own situations. Take the time to go through this section before you move onto the next chapter. Today, you learned about the amazing power of moving on and not living in the past.

Begin by using the 3 R's for handling the Past.

- **Rejoice** in what God did. List what God did and then thank Him.

_____

_____

- **Repent** for the wrong you did. List what you did wrong and then receive God's forgiveness in Jesus' name.

_____

_____

_____

- **Release** the hurts inflicted by others. List the hurts from others that you have now released.

_____

_____

_____

◇◇

Stop standing on the sidelines and get into the game!
In order to go on, you must get up!

◇◇

Review this list from the God of the Now, the New, and the Next. Check off those you have completed and then work on those you still need to deal with.

"   Stop sitting around complaining.
"   Stop standing around observing.

" Stop looking around for someone else to do something you should be doing.

" Stop waiting around for another train to come.

Are you ready to move on and trust Him with what's next?

Meditate on and Memorize:

> *Do not remember the former things,*
> *Nor consider the things of old.*
> *Behold, I will do a new thing,*
> *Now it shall spring forth;*
> *Shall you not know it?*
> *I will even make a road in the wilderness*
> *And rivers in the desert.*
> (Isaiah 43:18-19)

Declare: *Starting today, I will forget what's gone, appreciate what remains, and look forward to what's coming!*

Chapter 7

The Renewal of Being Changed in Christ...
Becoming New!

Do not remember the former things,
Nor consider the things of old.
*Behold, I will do a **new** thing, [I am changing things],*
Now it shall spring forth;
Shall you not know [perceive] it?
I will even make a road in the wilderness
And rivers in the desert.
(Isaiah 43:18-19 NKJV)

As we discovered in the last chapter, *new* is *cadash* and means new, fresh, and changed from something old to something new like a new song or a new spirit. The Message translation says, "Forget about what's happened; don't keep going over old history. Be alert, be present. I'm about to do something brand-new."

Change means that to do something new, you must let go of something old. Therefore, don't camp out in the past!

"Forget [don't obsess over; mull over and over again] the past..."

Don't let the past determine your future; God is your confidence... your future.

> *"Stop dwelling in the past;*
> *plan, process, and proceed toward God's future."*

2. ***Change*** will cost you time, money, and relationships.
Change Counts the Cost

> *For which of you, intending to build a tower, does not sit*
> *down first and count the cost, whether he has enough to*
> *finish it?* (Luke 14:28 NKJV)

3. ***Change*** requires new perspective, plans, process, and people.

A new perspective means you need to forget about what you want. You need to realize it's not about you. It's about what does God want? What is God's perspective and mindset?

> *"For My thoughts are not your thoughts, nor are your ways*
> *My ways," says the LORD. "For as the heavens are higher*
> *than the earth, so are My ways higher than your ways, and*
> *My thoughts than your thoughts."* (Isaiah 55:8-9 NKJV)

A new perspective leads you to new plans. You may have laid out a plan for your career, family, and future, but if it does not match up with God's plan, then it is all in vain.

> *Unless the Lord builds the house, they labor in vain who*
> *build it.* (Psalm 127:1 NKJV)

A new perspective and a new plan require a new process to achieve your God-given purpose. This process is most likely the most uncomfortable portion of changing to become who God destined you to be. It may require returning to the potter's wheel and having God do a major work inside you to create a vessel of great honor in His kingdom.

> *Then I went down to the potter's house, and there he was,*
> *making something at the wheel. And the vessel that he made*
> *of clay was marred in the hand of the potter; so he made it*
> *again into another vessel, as it seemed good to the potter to*
> *make.* (Jeremiah 18:3-4 NKJV)

> *But now, O LORD, You are our Father; We are the clay,*
> *and You our potter; And all we are the work of Your hand.*
> (Isaiah 64:8 NJV)

Many times, God will send people into your life to help guide you through the changes that will be necessary to accomplish His purpose for your life. It is important that we stay alert and continually ask the Lord who He wants to guide and mentor us. Not everyone in your life may be who God wants to help you.

4. *Change* demands focus.

Who/what is your focus?

> *Therefore, since we are surrounded by such a great cloud of witnesses, let us throw off everything that hinders and the sin that so easily entangles, and let us run with perseverance the race marked out for us. Let us fix our eyes on Jesus, the author and perfecter of our faith, who for the joy set before him endured the cross, scorning its shame, and sat down at the right hand of the throne of God.* (Hebrews 12:1-2 NIV)

5. *Change* precipitates a fight!

It has been said that when we are faced with the challenge of change, we have a choice to fight the obstacles that stand in our way or take flight and allow those people, events, or circumstances to prevent us from standing our ground.

> *Finally, be strong in the Lord and in his mighty power. Put on the full armor of God so that you can take your stand against the devil's schemes. For our struggle is not against flesh and blood, but against the rulers, against the authorities, against the powers of this dark world and against the spiritual forces of evil in the heavenly realms. Therefore put on the full armor of God, so that when the day of evil comes, you may be able to stand your ground, and after you have done everything, to stand.* (Ephesians 6:10-13)

6. *Change* requires following through and finishing the job!

You will mostly have to go where you have never been, do what you've never done before, and risk more than you ever have before to achieve the impossible and prosper beyond your wildest imaginations.

So, we must Focus, Fight, Finish!

I have fought the good fight, I have finished the race, I have kept the faith. (2 Timothy 4:7-8)

We must focus in our faith in God who has promised to never leave us or forsake us. In fact, we must fight the good fight of faith and finish the race.

7. **Change** involves a supportive group of friends, not just colleagues or associates. These are people who agree with you and will go with you! However, **change** requires that these are the right friends.

Blessed is the man who does not walk in the counsel of the wicked or stand in the way of sinners or sit in the seat of mockers. (Psalm 1:1)

8. **Change** demands three irrepressible forces: faith, hope, and love.

*And so **faith, hope, love** abide [**faith**—conviction and belief respecting man's relation to God and divine things; **hope**— joyful and confident expectation of eternal salvation; **love**— true affection for God and man, growing out of God's love for and in us], these three; but the greatest of these is love.* (1 Corinthians 13:13 AMP)

9. ***Change*** pushes us into God's presence and ceaseless prayer.

Moments of Release

You now have an opportunity to begin to apply the truths from God's Word presented in this powerful chapter to your own situations. Take the time to apply what you have learned about the amazing power of becoming changed in Christ and becoming new.

The Power of Being Changed in Christ means becoming more and more like Christ.

> *Now the Lord is that Spirit: and where the Spirit of the Lord is, there is liberty. But we all, with open face beholding as in a glass the glory of the Lord, are **changed** into the same image from glory to glory, even as by the Spirit of the Lord.* (2 Corinthians 3:17-18 KJV)

Change starts NOW!

- Stop procrastinating. Act in God's timing not your own.
- Don't be afraid. There is nothing to fear, nothing to lose, and nothing to hide when the faith of God fills you; the provision of God provides for you; and the light of God's forgiveness shines through you.
- Refuse to be distracted. Stay focused by fixing your eyes on Jesus, the author and finisher of your faith.
- Decide to trust and obey God. Believe God, forsake the world. Please Him not people!

- Focus...Fight...Finish Strong. Make this your declaration, "I will focus on Jesus; fight through and overcome every obstacle in His strength and finish every assignment God gives me.

Meditate on and Memorize: Hebrews 12:1-2

> *Therefore, since we are surrounded by such a great cloud of witnesses, let us throw off everything that hinders and the sin that so easily entangles, and let us run with perseverance the race marked out for us. Let us fix our eyes on Jesus, the author and perfecter of our faith, who for the joy set before him endured the cross, scorning its shame, and sat down at the right hand of the throne of God.* (Hebrews 12:1-2 NIV)

Declare: *I will focus, fight, and finish the race He has set before me!*

Final Word

The Right Way of Making Precise Decisions

I found out that for many that are new creations in Christ, it's hard for them to comprehend that God's ways and His thoughts are not our thoughts. It's essential to grasp this understanding because if you don't, you'll find yourself making wrong decisions based on your past experiences and education instead of making right decisions based on God's irrefutable or absolute truths in Scripture. Now, according to Josh McDowell in *Right vs. Wrong*, an irrefutable truth is right for all people, at all times, and in all situations. A myth or "relative truism" or "conventional wisdom" is what's right for some people, some of the time, and in some situations.

As our minds are being renewed by the power of the Holy Spirit and the Truths of Scripture, we must release ourselves from human opinions, religious clichés, family traditions, and actions that seek to please others instead of pleasing God. Before making any decision even one of posting on social media or watching/listening/reading any human-produced media, we must go through the wise and godly process of making precise decisions.

So, in this final word, I will equip you with the process for making precise decisions in life. I will teach you the four steps on how to make a precise decision.

First, you have to get over it. Too often you don't make precise decisions because you haven't gotten over the wrong ones you have made. Then you haven't gone beyond the wall that was there. It's time to get beyond it. Stop looking back to the wall, rut, or place where you were stuck... instead focus on Jesus, who is the answer.

Precise decisions are not based on human thoughts, feelings, or actions...

Remember it's not what we believe but who we trust that makes all the difference between right and wrong.

How do we make a precise decision? I want you to get it right for life, and it's a simple process, but you have to do it. Declare this, "My precise living and decision making starts now."

I am going to give you the four steps for making precise choices. These are critical steps. You have to understand these steps because if you don't go through these steps you are going to make wrong choices. Many of you know what's right, but you are making wrong choices because you don't process it correctly. I have learned about this process from a Lifeway curriculum called, *Truth Matters.*

Step 1: **Consider the choice.**

> *"The simple believes every word, but the prudent considers*
> *well his steps. A wise man fears and departs from evil, but*
> *a fool rages and is self-confident. A quick-tempered man acts*
> *foolishly, and a man of wicked intentions is hated."*
> (Proverbs 14:15-17)

Now the key word in this text is *consider.* "*Consider* the choice." It's being proactive instead of reactive. When something happens and you react to it, you will be foolish because you will react based on feelings, experience or based on your circumstances. And when you react, you are usually wrong.

Think about it. Somebody says something to you, and you just react to him or her. Usually what comes out is the flesh. And the reason the flesh comes out is because you are not proactive. You have not considered the choice before it happens. Being proactive is considering the choices ahead of you before you ever get there. Then if you get to a choice that you have not considered or instead of reacting to it, you step back, and you look at the whole picture.

Stop – Look–Listen. You learned that as a child. You need to do it as an adult.

Stop – Look–Listen. Don't make the decision yet. Look at the entire scope of the situation–particularly at the long-term consequences.

"If I say this or do this, how will this affect my life in five years?"

Every day is filled with choices. You must decide to follow God before the temptations arise. We must agree with Joshua at this point:

"...Serve the LORD! And if it seems evil to you to serve the LORD, choose for yourselves this day whom you will serve, ...But as for me and my house, we will serve the LORD" (Joshua 24:14-15).

If you don't consider the choices, you'll never became the person God wanted you to be.

If dealing with a sinful habit is a choice that's hindering you moving from your past, I urge you to deal with it quickly. One of A.W. Tozer's five spiritual vows is that you deal with sin quickly.

Consider the choice. Step back and look at all the options. Take the long look.

Consider the choice. Don't react quickly. Stop, look, and listen.

Step 2: Compare to God.

Here's the second step. Every day is going to be filled with choices. Let's go on. Choose this day–What are you going to do? Don't play the comparison game.

"What will others think? What will others do? Will others be upset with me?"

Others don't make any difference. You have to ask yourself, "Who am I trying to please?" And if you want to have a clue, the YouTube, streaming audio, or CD that some worship teams have recorded is *Audience of One.* You have just One in your audience on this one. His name is God.

"I wonder what my wife would think?"

Irrelevant.

"I wonder what my husband or my parents would think?"

It's of no consequence what they think. You are to live your life pleasing God and not men. So, you compare to God.

Notice this. I didn't say compare to Scripture. And the reason I didn't say to compare it to the Word is because when you start comparing it to the Word what happens is you become a legalist. I want to tell you something. Anybody who wants to play the con game can find any scripture in Bible to justify any action.

"Well, I murdered him because I went to the Bible. The Bible says that Cain killed Abel. It must be okay. It's in the Bible."

Remember these truths:

- Scripture can become rules and we become defense lawyers pleading our case.

- God is always right—absolute truths are biblical principles from the **whole counsel of God**. (Acts 20:27)
- We must stand on absolute truth not relativism.
- Absolute truth is what's true for all people, all times and in all situations.

And the LORD spoke to Moses, saying, "Speak to all the congregation of the children of Israel, and say to them: **'You shall be holy, for I the LORD your God am holy'**" (Leviticus 19:1-2).

Declare this, "I choose to be holy because God is holy."

The reason that you are pure isn't because you don't want to affect others or yourself with your sin. It's bigger than that. You are pure because God is pure. You are holy because God is holy. You are the temple of the Holy Spirit; do you not know it? The Spirit of God indwells you, and that means His character is in you.

Dr. Larry Keefauver, author of *Truth Matters*, tells this story...

I will never forget this. I asked my son Peter a question. We were working on a curriculum based on the book, Right From Wrong, and Peter walked through the room. I said, "Peter, I know you have made a decision to be pure before marriage–to have abstinence as your guideline. Why?"

He said, "Dad, are you writing a book?"

I said, "Yeah."

He said, "Am I going to be in the book?"

I said, "Yeah."

He said, "So, I've got to answer this right?"

I say, "Of course."

"Because the Bible says, 'flee immorality.'"

"Great, Peter," I replied. "Why else?"

"Because I want to save my purity for my wife."

"Wonderful," I answered. "Why else?"

"Because if you found out I wasn't pure, you'd kill me!" he shouted and walked out of the room.

I explained later to Peter that the reason he stayed pure was that God was pure and holy. The living God lived in him. Therefore, his desire to be holy and pure came from God Himself.

Step 3: Choose the right.

When you know what is right and don't do it, it's sin (James 4:17). When we know what the right is, we must NOT procrastinate or make excuses. We must ACT! Listen to what God says:

"I call heaven and earth as witnesses today against you, that I have set before you life and death, blessing and cursing; **therefore choose life,** that both you and your descendants may live; that you may love the LORD your God, that you may obey His voice, and that you may cling to Him, for He is your life and the length of your days" (Deuteronomy 30:19-20).

So what keeps us from choosing what's right?

- **Ignorance** (We perish for lack of knowledge.)
- **Rebellion** (I do what I want.)
- **Fear** (I fear risk & change, so I choose comfort, relief and consequences.)
- **The Past** (I can't let go of the past in order to grasp God's future & hope.)
- **Procrastination** (I'll wait just a bit longer and see what may happen.)

All these things can keep you from choosing what is right. I want to just give you a quick list.

Ignorance. You don't know what's right. People perish because of a lack of knowledge. I want to tell you something. When you have a decision to make, Bishop, Pastor, Elder or Minister will not be there whispering in your ear. You are going to have to know the Bible for yourself. You are going to have to know God for yourself. You are going to have to get it right. It's between you and God right now.

Rebellion. Some of you are just plain out rebellious. The reason you make wrong decisions is because you are rebelling against God. He is asking for your obedience in this matter.

Fear. Some of you can't do what's right because you are fearful. You fear risk and change, and so you choose comfort and relief, and then you suffer the consequences. Most of you don't like repentance because it hurts. You have got to change. So, you ask or pray for relief, and you never change. You want God to be a Tylenol instead of a surgeon. You want a quick fix and not a lifestyle change.

The Past and Procrastination. Some of you are still in the past and a few of you love to procrastinate. You can do the right thing at the wrong time and have a huge mess on your hands–a huge problem on your plate. Right?

The Holy Spirit gives you the power to overcome hindrances to doing what's right. Let Him empower you to choose the right!

Step 4: Count the cost!

"For which of you, intending to build a tower, does not sit down first and **count the cost**, whether he has enough to finish it" (Luke 14:28).

After we choose the right, we must count the cost. No man builds a tower who doesn't first sit down and count the cost whether he has enough to finish it or not. Every right decision will cost you something.

So, when I have a decision to make, I am going to consider the choice. I am going to step back. I am going to look at it. I am going to take the long look. Then I am going to compare my options to God and choose what reflects His character, His holiness, His grace, His truth, and His purity. Then I am going to move on, and I am going to do it. Just do the right thing! Some believers are missing the season of their blessing because they are procrastinating and not doing the right thing now.

And finally, I am going to count the cost. I am willing to pay the price. I don't care what it costs me. I don't care what the sacrifice is. I may lose everything, but I will lose it all to gain Him.

"For whosoever will save his life shall lose it; but whosoever shall lose his life for my sake and the gospel's, the same shall save it.

For what shall it profit a man, if he shall gain the whole world, and lose his own soul?

Or what shall a man give in exchange for his soul?" (Mark 8:35-37 KJV)

It's time, right now, for you to get over it...

So that you can get beyond it...

In order to get it right for the rest of your life by making right decisions!

I remember watching one of my favorite Pastors (Dr. Jamal Bryant) go through public humiliation dealing with adultery and scandals. Dr. Jamal Bryant was the Pastor of Empowerment Temple A.M.E. Church in Baltimore, MD. It was recorded that he started with ten members and grew it to over ten thousand members in less than ten years. Empowerment Temple was considered one of the fastest growing churches in the country.

I admired Dr. Bryant's approach to the text and his charismatic preaching, but I was deeply hurt when he talked about his infidelities that ruined his marriage and crippled his church. After he came public with this information, many pastors and leaders turned their backs on Dr. Bryant. His itinerary didn't have as many assignments due to his lack of making the wrong choices.

After admitting his wrong and deciding to make the choice of working on himself, God gave Dr. Bryant another chance of making an impact in the lives of others. Pastor Jamal Bryant then leaving his church that he founded in Baltimore went to Pastor New Birth Baptist Church in Lithonia, Georgia. Many wondered how could a man that made many bad choices in life could rebound and Pastor a mega church with over 25,000 members. As I was writing this book and researching this four-step process, I can understand how releasing your past and moving forward worked in the favor of this pastor.

Dr. Jamal Bryant moved past the fear of what others thought of him and totally made the confession to please God. I will never forget hearing a radio interview that he had when he moved to the state of Georgia. The radio announcer asked him this question, "How can you push pass the bad choices you have made in life?"

His response blessed me, and I pray that it blesses you. Pastor Bryant's response was, "I simply pray this prayer, Lord your will, nothing more, nothing less and nothing else."

As I close, I simply want to say this prayer with you, and I want you to use this as well to be proactive in making precise decisions. "Lord your will, nothing more, nothing less, and nothing else."

Endnotes

1   Published October 12th 2004 by Faithwords (first published October 1st 2004)

2   www.brainyquote.com/quotes/mark_twain_131203

3   https://www.linkedin.com/pulse/stuck-rut-get-out-grave-terry-daniel/

4   www.brainyquote.com/.../martin-luther-king-jr-quotes

5   genius.com/Mahalia-jackson-if-i-can-help.

6   Cook, Suzan Johnson. *Moving Up* The Crown Publishing Group. Kindle Edition.

7   ttps://www.crosswalk.com/faith/spiritual-life/inspiring-quotes/30-inspiring-christian-quotes.html

8   https://www.crosswalk.com/faith/spiritual-life/inspiring-quotes/40-powerful-quotes-from-corrie-ten-boom.html

9   ttps://www.crosswalk.com/faith/spiritual-life/inspiring-quotes/30-inspiring-christian-quotes.html

10   https://www.goodreads.com/author/quotes/1082290.A_W_Tozer

11   Dr. Larry Keefauver, *The 77 Irrefutable Truths of Ministry*

12   *Joan Winmill Brown, ed.,* The Martyred Christian *(New York, NY: Macmillan, 1985), 157.*

13   Adapted from https://www.christianbiblereference.org/faq_ChristianValues.htm

14   https://www.goodreads.com/work/
     quotes/29986-the-bait-of-satan-living-free-from-the-deadly-trap-of-offense

CPSIA information can be obtained
at www.ICGtesting.com
Printed in the USA
LVHW080311191120
671844LV00038B/11

9 781632 218759